CRYPTOCURRENCY: COMPLETE BASICS GUIDE FOR BEGINNERS TO TRADING AND INVESTING IN BITCOIN, ETHEREUM, ALTCOINS, LITECOIN, RIPPLE, AND OTHERS

BY

Rick Maverick

DISCLAIMER

The information presented in this book solely and fully represents the views of the author as of the date of publication. Any omission, or potential misrepresentation of, any peoples or companies, is entirely unintentional. As a result of changing information, conditions or contexts, this author reserves the right to alter content at his sole discretion impunity.

The book is for informational and advertising purposes only and while every attempt has been made to verify the information contained herein, the author assumes no responsibility for errors, inaccuracies, and omissions. Each person has unique needs and this book cannot take these individual differences into account. For ease of use, all links in this book are redirected through the link to facilitate any future changes and minimize dead links.

TABLE OF CONTENTS

INTRODUCTION

Growing up is scary. Going from not having a care in the world to taking care of everything by yourself can be a daunting task. Just paying the bills and buying groceries is enough, but when you start to think about savings and investment portfolios, the adult world can become overwhelming.

There's your retirement fund—known as a 401K—at your job, of course. However, understanding how your 401K makes money can be a little confusing. Once you start thinking about how to invest your savings without help, personal finances can become a formidable proposition.

The rise of cryptocurrencies such as Bitcoin, as well as safe ways to invest in them, has led to an intriguing financial opportunity – cryptocurrency-based investment funds. With the popularity of cryptocurrencies many investors are now trying to determine how to invest into this new asset class.

As with any investment into a new technology, there are many factors to consider when assessing their future. To make an informed decision, one must look at the origins of the technology as well as the potential applications and limitations in the foreseeable future.

It is easy to see that cryptocurrencies like Bitcoin or Ethereum are fascinating subjects that are becoming more and more popular. Understanding these new digital currencies, how we can use them in our daily lives, and how they will affect global commerce are extremely important timely topics. If you have managed to avoid using cryptocurrency thus far, or you are a late adopter in general, not to worry.

After reading this book, you will jump right into the cryptocurrency frenzy, and you will be glad you did. So, you've been hearing all the buzz about cryptocurrencies and want to know what you're missing. You've heard of Bitcoin, Ethereum, Litecoin, Ripple and a whole slew of alternate cryptocurrencies but have no idea what they're all about. Well, you've picked the right book. I have put together the information you need to get started.

Important disclaimer: Trading cryptocurrencies is highly risky due to high volatility of prices of most coins. Constantly profitable trading is not impossible, yet it requires continuous studying of candlestick charts, oscillators and indicators; researching through the technologies behind various cryptos to determine the most promising ones; and following up news related to adoption, protocol updates and mainstream mentions. Always try to trade only what you can afford to lose, until you develop the necessary skills and knowledge to risk a larger capital.

WHAT IS CRYPTOCURRENCY?

Cryptocurrency is a type of digital currency that is based on cryptography. Cryptocurrency uses cryptography for security, making it difficult to counterfeit. Public and private keys are often used to transfer the currency from one person to another.

Cryptocurrency is considered a counter-culture movement. Cryptocurrency is essentially a fiat currency, which means it only has value if people agree to such and use it as a medium of exchange. However, because it is not tied to any country, its value cannot be affected by a central bank. In the case of Bitcoin, the most prominent functioning example of cryptocurrency, its value is determined by supply and demand in the market. As such, this currency behaves much like gold and other precious metals.

The Economics of Cryptocurrency

Algorithmic Governance

Rules for what are considered valid cryptocurrency transactions are embedded in the peer-to-peer software that cryptocurrency miners and users run. One valid kind of transaction is the creation of new coins out of thin air. Not everyone can execute this kind of transaction – miners compete for the right to execute one of these transactions per block (on Bitcoin, every ten minutes or so). When a miner discovers a valid hash for a block, they can claim the new coins.

A transaction in which a miner claims new coins, like any other transaction, has to conform to the expectations of the network. The network will reject a block that contains a transaction in which a miner awards themselves too many new coins. The growth of coins is limited by a pre-determined amount per block.

On Bitcoin, the pre-determined amount is not scheduled to be constant over time but rather is set to halve every 210,000 blocks, or about every four years, as described above. The total supply of bitcoins will asymptotically approach but never exceed, 21 million. It will reach 20 million in 2025 and stop growing altogether in 2140.

Open Source Governance

The astute reader will note that the Bitcoin software that enforces particular rules about valid transactions and the rate of money creation does not appear out of thin air. Rather, the rules embedded in the software emerge from an interplay between leaders of the open source project that manages what is known as the 'reference client,' other developers, miners, the user community and malicious actors. The dynamic between these players is as crucial to understanding

Bitcoin as that of central banks, traditional monetary institutions and monetary politics are to understanding fiat currency.

Bitcoin, like all other even moderately successful cryptocurrencies to date, is a non-proprietary open source project. Users tend to look with suspicion on cryptocurrency projects that are closed source, which features significant pre-mining to reward insiders, or that have other proprietary features. Other expectations of the user community also impose a check on developers. For example, the hard cap of 21 million bitcoins, while in principle subject to change through a software update, appears to be non-negotiable for Bitcoin, although other cryptocurrencies have different money supply rules.

Blockchain Technology

The blockchain is a ledger, or list, of all of a cryptocurrency's transactions, and is the technology underlying Bitcoin and other cryptocurrencies. This decentralized public ledger keeps a record of all transactions that take place across the peer-to-peer network. Users can contribute to the network by providing computational power to assist with the verification of transactions in real time (known as "mining").

This technology allows market participants to transfer assets across the Internet without the need for a central third party. Specifically, the buyer and seller interact directly with each other, and there is no need for verification by a trusted third-party intermediary. Identifying information is encrypted, and no personal information is shared. However, a transaction record is created. For this reason, transactions are considered pseudonymous, not anonymous.

The blockchain public ledger technology has the potential to disrupt a wide variety of transactions, in addition to the traditional payments system. These include stocks, bonds, and other financial assets for which records are stored digitally and for which currently there is a need for a trusted third party to provide verification of the transaction.

Chain Reaction

For its first five years of existence, Bitcoin overshadowed its engine in technological circles, as the price of one coin fluctuated from nothing to $31, to $2, to $266, to $100, to $1,250, to $200 and so on.

The blockchain, intended to document bitcoin transactions, can also be used as a distributed ledger for; well, anything. If it can be recorded digitally, it can be written on a blockchain and kept beyond the reach of controlling states, malicious attackers and those who would rewrite history.

Initially, this took the form of what became known as "colored coins." The idea was that a particular sliver of bitcoin could be permanently marked with some other property: say, ownership of stock, or a plot of land. It can be thought of as taking a marker and writing on a £5 note: "Whoever holds this also owns one common share of Apple stock" – except that thanks to modern cryptography, the signature cannot be forged, the £5 cannot be falsified, and everyone can see when it changes hands.

For a long time, the ability to use the blockchain in this way was treated as an interesting side-effect of bitcoin's role as a currency. But the tenfold collapse in the currency during 2014 prompted many who had invested in the bitcoin ecosystem – whether financially or intellectually – to seek other uses for the underlying technology.

London's Provenance, for instance, aimed to use the same technology to provide a transparent, trustworthy platform for presenting the history and, well, the provenance of a business's products. The company has gone through some changes since it was launched in 2013, and the blockchain now forms a core part of its offering. The idea is that a Chilean vineyard can, for instance, publicly share a bottle's origin in its fields, and track it throughout the chain of production, all the while recording its statements publicly for posterity. At the end of the chain, a shopper can check a tag on the bottle and find out precisely what happened on its journey.

Others aim to preserve the financial core of the blockchain concept while returning some establishment credibility to the project. In May 2015, New York's Nasdaq announced it was exploring the potential of using colored coins to track stocks. Nasdaq's head, Bob Greifeld, was optimistic, saying: "Utilising the blockchain is a natural digital evolution for managing physical securities. Once you cut the apron strings of the need for the physical, the opportunities we can envision blockchain providing a stand to benefit not only our clients but the broader global capital markets."

It is also becoming clear that it will no longer be accurate to talk about "the" blockchain. Instead, there are many blockchains, as companies are born with different needs from a distributed ledger than those of Bitcoin. Perhaps the most innovative of them is Russian-Swiss company Ethereum, formed around the idea of using the same sort of network to do much more than record information.

Created by Vitalik Buterin in 2013, the Ethereum network allows users to create "smart contracts" that can automatically be executed by any computer running the Ethereum software in exchange for the network's currency, "ether," creating one gigantic distributed computer for hire. Advocates insist the idea could change the world of computing, allowing for digital smart locks that open when a fee is paid, or letting musicians release songs for collaborators to rebuild in real time.

Ethereum gained its biggest public exposure following the creation of a smart contract, called the Decentralized Autonomous Organization (DAO), intended to be a sort of crowdsourced hedge fund. Investors could buy into it, and vote on where the pool of cash it controlled was invested, before splitting their share of the pool and cashing out. But there was a major flaw in the code behind it: it was possible to write an infinite loop of cash-out instructions, taking your share of the DAO out over and over again. One user noticed this early, and managed to steal $50m worth of ether before the flow was stemmed.

More generally, the undeniable potential of the blockchain has led to it becoming one of the tech's newest buzzwords. Companies with little good reason to use a distributed ledger, throw it in their business plan anyway, in the hope of getting an extra $25m from venture capitalists eager to cash in on the trend.

Even for those uses where it can be transformative, blockchain technology still comes with its downsides. The mining process that underpins the whole technology is a colossal waste of energy, for one thing.

More fundamentally, sometimes centralization can be a good thing: the card company can reverse a fraudulent credit card transaction, but stolen bitcoins are gone forever.

Both the potential and the risk are only gradually becoming evident, as is illustrated by the case of the Decentralised Autonomous Organisation known simply as the DAO. The idea, in a nutshell, is a company in which funders initially invested in return for voting rights, but which would then operate simply through "smart contracts" running on a blockchain and implemented via software. The DAO was launched to considerable excitement, having raised more than $150m in a digital currency known as "ether," but it was almost immediately hacked, with approximately a third of the ether taken. It is a cautionary tale. In the scale of its ambition, it also helps to explain why some see blockchain technology as almost on the scale of the world wide web.

Don and Alex Tapscott got in early on this "revolution." The father and son team are well positioned: Don Tapscott's 15 books include The Digital Economy (1994) and Wikinomics (2006); Alex Tapscott is the CEO and founder of an advisory firm building blockchain companies. Their book features interviews with leading figures in tech, business, and academia, presented in a highly accessible form.

Blockchain Revolution aims to provide a broad overview of changes the technology could bring about. Since the Tapscotts have a penchant for numbered lists, I'll give four of their examples. First, they suggest, blockchain technology could transform remittances, the largest flow of funds into the developing world; transfers could take place in an hour rather than a week, and with the greatly reduced commission. Second, the technology could provide immutable land title registration for the estimated 7.6 billion people in the world who have only a tenuous right to their land. Third, it could overhaul online identity, allowing us greater privacy but also the ability to gain value from those aspects of our data we are prepared to share. Finally, blockchain technology could help artists and musicians claim ownership of their work and receive a fair share of its value – no mean feat in the digital era.

Overall, the shift the Tapscotts envisage – from hierarchies to networks, and towards a new era of "distributed capitalism" – sounds appealing. But each of the four examples mentioned above, like the numerous others in the book, raises the same two questions. Is this blockchain revolution likely? And is it desirable? In answer to the first question, the Tapscotts acknowledge barriers to adoption, particularly in the chapter on "showstoppers." As regards the second, they allude to the possible dystopian consequences as well as the utopian. At one point they suggest that blockchain technology could, if we get it wrong, allow institutions to entrench their wealth, provide a platform for a new kind of surveillance society, and even, together with related technological advances, get out of control and turn against humans. (The DAO attack, which took place after the Tapscotts finished their book, was not an example of this – there was a human hacker or hackers behind it – but is, perhaps, an early warning of the dangers of placing too much faith in code.)

Bitcoin And Its Bright Future

Transactions Beyond Borders

Bitcoin does not discriminate against anyone due to their background. Bitcoin will make sure that you get the money through to anything you want. Sometimes, there are laws which prevent you from buying something from a particular country. These kinds of issues come up all the time. Imagine how Bitcoin facilitates lives of rich people with loads of money.

Foolproof Cyber Security Measures

You can use the blockchain in Bitcoin to look at the most recent transactions taking place. All you need is internet access to search for the record of the Bitcoin history. The users of Bitcoin can easily choose between going public or completely hiding their privacy. This way they can choose the way they like to use this cryptocurrency. You do not need to identify yourself to the Bitcoin protocol. There are no compliance requirements to meet.

No Inflation No Heartbreaks

No matter which currency you try to store, it has that inflation impact on it. Inflation is a result of many micro and macroeconomic factors affecting a country.

A Truly Global Currency

Bitcoin is a truly global currency which does not consider where you live, who you are, and what you do. It is available to everyone who has a potential use for it. The peer-to-peer method ensures that you directly get the money into your account. You do not have to report to any third party or financial institution. And, you can send as much as you would like to.

Bitcoin has impacted much on the currency arena. It can be easily utilized to purchase merchandise anonymously. It also provides the benefits of easy and cheap international payments and is not subjected or limited to any country or regulation.

Some people see Bitcoin as a vehicle for investments and buy Bitcoin by trusting that they will increase in value. To get Bitcoins, you can purchase on an Exchange marketplace that allows people buy or sell them, utilizing other various currencies. The transferring of Bitcoins is easily done by forwarding Bitcoins to one another person utilizing mobile apps or their PCs online. It's just like sending cash digitally.

Valuable Secure Asset

With Bitcoins, you have a currency value that can be stored in what's called a "digital wallet," which subsists either within the cloud or on a computer. This digital wallet is like a virtual bank account that lets account holders within it send or receive Bitcoins, purchase goods and services or store them.

Although the FDIC insures most bank accounts, Bitcoin wallets are not, yet they are safe, secure and have payment flexibility benefits. Unlike the US dollar, gold, silver, or some other precious metals, Bitcoins are scarce, and this scarcity is algorithmic.

Regarding international remittance, Bitcoin is a winner. There is no worry about fraud or security. At some money exchange businesses, for instance, migrant workers could utilize Bitcoin to send payments from one nation to another via email.

On the 27th of June in 2014, the US Government was scheduled to auction off about 30,000 BTC that was confiscated from the shutdown of Silk Road, an online black market operation. At that time, the value of Bitcoins was 633.84 dollars.

If you take a good look at some of the local merchants downtown, the inner cities or online, you will see the Bitcoin logo acceptance in the window or on the door.

Bitcoin is still maturing and is making a tremendous progression towards being one of the most sensible currencies ever created.

Bitcoins can be sent, received and managed through various independent websites, PC clients, and mobile device software.

There are a variety of ways to acquire bitcoins:

- ❖ Accept bitcoins as payment for goods or services.
- ❖ There are several services where you can trade them for traditional currency.
- ❖ Find someone to trade cash for bitcoins in-person through a local directory.
- ❖ Participate in a mining pool.

Bitcoin doesn't ask that it users trust any institution. Its security is based on the cryptography that is an integral part of its structure, and that is readily available for any and all to see. Instead of one entity keeping track of transactions, the entire network does, so Bitcoins are astoundingly difficult to steal, or double-spend. Bitcoins are created regularly and predictably, and by many different users, so no one can decide to make a whole lot more and lessen their value. In short, Bitcoin is designed to be inflation-proof, double-spend-proof and completely distributed.

Bitcoins are still far from mainstream, but they can be used as a valid form of payment for all kinds of goods and services.

One advantage Bitcoin fans cite is the ability to move money instantly anywhere in the world. By eliminating the middlemen -- credit-card companies, financial institutions, PayPal -- Bitcoin allows money to change hands digitally as quickly as cash does in the real world.

Buying Bitcoins from individuals with Paypal is possible, but requires the seller to have some trust that the buyer will not file a claim with PayPal to reverse the payment.

Bitcoin markets are competitive -- meaning the price of a bitcoin will rise or fall depending on supply and demand at certain price levels. Only a fraction of bitcoins issued to date are found in the exchange markets for sale. So even though technically a buyer with lots of money could buy all the bitcoins offered for sale unless those holding the rest of the bitcoins offer them for sale as well, even the wealthiest, most determined buyer can't get at them.

Additionally, new currency continues to be issued daily and will continue to do so for decades though over time the rate at which they are issued declined to insignificant levels.

Those who are mining aren't obligated to sell their bitcoins, so not all bitcoins will make it to the markets even.

This situation doesn't suggest, however, that the markets aren't vulnerable to price manipulation. It doesn't take significant amounts of money to move the market price up or down, and thus Bitcoin remains a volatile asset.

Alt(ernative) Coins

Alternative coins or alt-coins are cryptocurrencies that copy many of the features of Bitcoin. Most of the alt-coins are based on Bitcoin's source code with some changes.

As Bitcoin's code is released under an open source license, it is acceptable to take a copy of the code, modify it, and release a new cryptocurrency. Many developers have done exactly that, creating many alt-coins.

Development in Bitcoin has been conservative and value-preserving, focusing on avoiding the introduction of errors. On the other hand, alt-coins often do not have the restrictions of a production system like Bitcoin, or the requirement of backward compatibility, allowing them to test new tweaks and features. However, Bitcoin can opt-in some of these features if the developers consider them worthy.

One controversial feature of some alt-coins has been pre-mining. Pre-mining refers to the fact that the developers of some alt-coins kept a large portion of the coins before the launch. The often-cited rationale for pre-mining is to create a reserve to pay developers to maintain and extend the alt-coin. However, a large percentage of pre-mined tokens is often counterproductive as it deters potential users, thus thwarting adoption.

Alt-coins can suffer from a multipool entering their network. Multipools are mining pools that switch from one alt-coin to another opportunistically, always mining the most profitable alt-coin at the time. Mining profitability depends on the alt-coin's mining difficulty and its exchange rate. A multipool can create wild fluctuations in the mining difficulty of an alt-coin because when a multipool enters an alt-coin, it drives the mining difficulty higher. Once this multipool leaves the alt-coin, it can take a long time to revert to the original mining difficulty.

Note that alt-coins are often distinguished from meta-coins such as Counterparty, Ethereum, or Ripple. Alt-coins commonly refer to currencies whose implementation is a fork of the Bitcoin source code with some tweaks, while meta-coins refer to new implementations from scratch (or layers on top of Bitcoin such as Counterparty or Mastercoin) that add features, such as support for digital assets, not available in Bitcoin currently. This distinction is somewhat tenuous, and the terms alt-coin and meta-coin are sometimes used interchangeably.

Litecoin (LTC) is arguably the most successful alt-coin. It was released in 2011 and as of the time of writing had a market capitalization of roughly 5% of that of Bitcoin (It is sometimes referred to as "silver to Bitcoin's gold.")

The differences introduced in Litecoin compared to Bitcoin are:

It uses scrypt as its proof-of-work algorithm. Scrypt is a memory hard key-derivation function introduced by Colin Percival. A memory-hard function requires a reasonably large amount of Random Access Memory (RAM) to be evaluated. This implements in special purpose hardware, i.e., ASICs, less efficient because it requires some die area to be reserved for memory. In the words of Colin Percival, the creator of scrypt, "the point of scrypt is to limit how many hashes you can compute per second per mm2 of ASIC".

Block generation time is targeted at 2.5 minutes, which makes for the faster inclusion of transactions in a block. Note that faster inclusion time should not be interpreted as faster confirmations. The security of a transaction in the blockchain depends on the computational effort spent in mining the blocks which are on top of the block that includes the transaction. Assuming the network hash rate stays constant, a lower block generation time makes the mining difficulty of each block lower and thus does not have any effect on the security of a transaction over time. There is, however, an advantage to lower block generation times because inclusion in a first block is usually enough security for low-value transactions.

The main idea behind scrypt is that it generates a lot of pseudorandom numbers that it stores in RAM so they can be accessed on demand. The algorithm then accesses this memory in a pseudo-random fashion some times before returning the result. An implementation where no RAM is used is possible. In this case, the pseudo-random numbers would be generated as needed. However, as the generation of these pseudo-random numbers is computationally intensive, and the numbers are accessed several times, it is computationally very costly to compute scrypt this way. This scrypt follows a marked time-memory trade-off. The parameters of the scrypt algorithm can be tweaked to require more or less RAM and computing power. However, the implementation of scrypt used in Litecoin is somewhat watered down, requiring only 128kB of memory, allegedly not to stress too much the computers of users running non-mining nodes. This parameterization of scrypt makes it possible to implement Litecoin mining in ASICs, although still less efficiently than Bitcoin in ASICs: it is estimated that a factor of 10 reduces the ASIC advantage in Litecoin compared to Bitcoin.

Scrypt is a cryptographic algorithm that has received much less scrutiny by cryptographers than the SHA256 hash function. This makes it in some ways a riskier choice as the chances that vulnerability is found are higher.

The main advantages of a memory-hard proof-of-work function are:

It can increase the number of miners as everybody with a computer has an equal chance of mining, in contrast with Bitcoin mining, which requires specialized equipment. Having many small miners, proponents argue, provides greater network resilience.

It can lead to lower resource waste compared to regular proof-of-work. In particular, a lot of resources were invested in early mining equipment for Bitcoin that was later put to rest because the mining technology made them obsolete.

The main arguments against memory-hard functions are that all functions will eventually be implemented in ASICs and that if mining is done using PCs, then a large portion of mining will be done by botnets, i.e., armies of compromised computers.

The mining reward in Litecoin is kept the same as Bitcoin's, i.e., 50 coins per block, halving roughly every 4 years and leading to a maximum supply of 84 million litecoins, or 4 times the money supply of Bitcoin.

As the mining algorithm is different, the hash rate of Litecoin is not directly comparable to that of Bitcoin, i.e., Litecoin's GH/s are not comparable to Bitcoin's GH/s. Comparisons of the relative security of both networks have to take into account the relative cost of the hardware required to pull off double-spending attacks.

Litecoin has benefited from the migration of Bitcoin mining to ASICs, as many early Bitcoin miners have re-purposed their hardware, CPUs first and then GPUs, to mine Litecoin. The fact that Litecoin uses scrypt, which is more ASIC-resistant than

SHA256^2, is perceived as an advantage by enthusiast miners.

Litecoin

Litecoins are a form of cryptocurrency that has grown in popularity in response to the demand for alternative currency options from consumers around the world. This currency works much like standard world currencies. Traders and investors have realized the great potential this currency has to offer, and it is heavily traded by beginning and seasoned investors alike. The best way to get the most out of Litecoin trades is to utilize the services of a Litecoin broker. There are numerous Litecoin brokers available that have excellent reputations for providing their clients with superb service. These brokers will be able to help traders make sound decisions about their investments

When you hire a good Litecoin broker, they will have numerous tools and resources available to ensure that your trades go smoothly. Perhaps the most used tool by these brokers is the Litecoin news widget. This widget can be fully customized to meet your specific needs. It will give continual updates on cryptocurrency news and other relevant information so that you will be privy to the latest news developments as they are released on the wires.

What are Litecoins?

Litecoins are a form of virtual currency that can be obtained and used to buy and sell various services and products such as jewelry, clothing, food, and electronics. Since this currency is only used online, its value is determined by demand on currency trading websites. This cryptocurrency can be traded, or it can be mined. When mining for the currency, the process can be a daunting task. Computers solved mathematical equations, and they are rewarded as a result. Nearly any good computer can mine for the currency, but statistically, the odds of success are low, and it can take days just to earn a couple of coins.

The Difference between Litecoins and Bitcoins

The main difference is that Litecoins can be purchased much faster than Bitcoins, and their limit is set to 84 million, whereas Bitcoin's limit is only 21 million in comparison. Bitcoins are accepted at more online stores, but Litecoins are being risen in popularity every single day. The currency is decentralized, so this is a great advantage to traders. The cost is predicted to be lower than Bitcoin costs, as the cryptocurrency becomes more widely known.

Dogecoin

Dogecoin (DOGE) was introduced in 2013. Dogecoin is a straightforward fork of Litecoin. Its main innovation lies in its marketing strategy. It associates with the famous internet doge meme, transmitting a message of light-headedness and fun that will hopefully cater to a wider demographic than other cryptocurrencies.

On the technical side, Dogecoin targets a block generation time of 1 minute. The supply of dogecoins is frontloaded with 98 billion dogecoins entering circulation during its first year, and a fixed 5.2 billion in subsequent years (Wikipedia, 2014f). Thus Doge-coin is inflationary (5% increase in the supply during its second year), but its rate of inflation decreases over time5. According to its supporters, this large supply of dogecoins breaks the psychological barrier of spending or giving them away, with the result that Dogecoin is widely used as a tipping system.

Peercoin

Peercoin (PPC) was introduced in 2012. Its main innovation is that it uses a hybrid proof-of-stake/proof-of-work system. In a proof-of-stake system, new blocks are minted—analogous to mining—by holders of coins in proportion to how many coins they control. Proof-of-stake does not involve solving a partial hash inversion problem and thus requires minimal electricity consumption. For this reason, it is argued that Peercoin is a green alternative to Bitcoin.

In Peercoin there are two types of blocks, those generated with proof-of-stake and those generated with proof-of-work. Blocks generated under proof-of-work follow similar rules to Bitcoin's block generation. However, the block reward for proof-of-work halves every time the difficulty increases 16 times .

Blocks generated under proof-of-stake are awarded to transaction outputs in a manner that is proportional to their coin age. Coin age is the product of the number of coins in the transaction output multiplied by the time since those funds were last spent. The protocol that awards a new block to a particular transaction outputs proceeds as follows:

First, a transaction called coinstake (similar to Bitcoin's coinbase) is created. This transaction spends the funds in the transaction output, destroying its coin age. Then a hash of a header that includes this transaction and the time (in seconds since 1970) is computed.

This hash is then checked against a proof-of-work requirement, whose difficulty is inverse to the coin age. Note that only one hash per second per transaction output is computed, a very low computational load.

If the hash matches the proof-of-work requirement, the user in control of the transaction output can mint a new proof-of-stake block and receive the block reward.

The proof-of-work system also uses coin age to determine the security of the blockchain: in case of a fork, the branch that consumes more coin age is the correct one. Initially, proof-of-work is used in Peercoin, but over time proof-of-stake becomes the primary source of coin generation, as the block reward for proof-of-work blocks diminishes.

Transaction fees are fixed at 0.01 PPC, but unlike Bitcoin, these fees are destroyed. Users minting blocks are solely compensated through the block reward. The proof-of-stake block reward is set at a 1% annual rate. Thus, in the long run, the inflation will be 1% minus the fees destroyed.

Initial versions of Peercoin included checkpointing, i.e., the inclusion of hash values of certain blocks in the software releases, as a protection against attacks. It is planned that this practice will be phased out in the short future.

Namecoin

Namecoin (NMC) is both a crypto-currency and a decentralized key/value store. This decentralized key/value store is used to implement an alternative Domain Name System (DNS). The DNS is the piece of the internet infrastructure that enable human-read-able addresses to be resolved to IP addresses1. The internet DNS is under the control of ICANN. Namecoin implements an alternative DNS using the .bit top-level domain.

The Namecoin protocol adds new transactions to interact with the key/value store: name_new and name_firstupdate3. These transactions create a new key/value. Any piece of data can be registered in Namecoin's key/value store. If the key happens to start with "d/," it is considered a .bit domain. For instance, registering "d/understanding bitcoin" would register the domain understandingbitcoin.bit. name_update. This transaction allows a user to renew a name, paying a (small) fee. An update transaction can also be used to change the value of the key/value pair, such as changing the IP address associated with a domain name. An update transaction also allows transferring a name from one Namecoin address to another. Names registered in Namecoin expire after 36,000 blocks, approximately 250 days if no update is seen.

Users running a Namecoin node have a full copy of the key/value store and can access it at any time. Or some users might prefer to connect to a Name-coin node and query the node for specific information, much in the same way that an SPV wallet queries a full Bitcoin node.

Other Namecoin settings are kept at their default Bitcoin values: proof-of-work function is SHA256^2, block generation targets 10 minutes, block reward starts at 50 namecoins and halves every 4 years, the final monetary base will be 21 million namecoins, and so on. Namecoin allows merge-mining with Bitcoin after a change in the protocol in 2011.

A traditional DNS domain registration is associated with a name and physical address. In contrast, a Namecoin .bit domain registration is only linked to a Namecoin address, whose private key has control over the domain. Thus changes to a domain or transfers of domains between two addresses can be done pseudonymously. Advocates of Namecoin also argue that its decentralized nature makes censorship of domain names much more difficult. Other advantages over traditional DNS is that it is cheaper, faster, and more secure4. Other applications of Namecoin are an ID name-space (for storing contact information), a messaging system, a web of trust, or a notary.

Auroracoin

Auroracoin, the cryptocurrency created by the pseudonymous Icelander Baldur Friggjar Óðinsson (who may be a group or an individual), was created as a national alternative currency for Iceland. The creator or creators intended the alternative currency to give a boost to Iceland's economy and allow for a way around tight capital controls. Unlike many cryptocurrencies, Auroracoin was pre-mined before it went public, then, the "airdrop" commenced, and each citizen of

Iceland became eligible to claim 31.8 Auroracoins free of charge.

Auroracoin was launched in February, and ten million Auroracoins were pre-mined before launch date. The airdrop began on a Monday when all 330,000 people listed in Iceland's national ID database became eligible for claiming 31.8 Auroracoin. The creator(s) intend to give half of all Auroracoins to be created to all the citizens of Iceland free of charge, and Iceland's national ID database makes that task rather easy.

Auroracoin was created to allow the citizens of Iceland to get around tight capital controls set in 2008 by Iceland's Central Bank in response to the global economic crisis. The controls prevent the króna (Iceland's currency) from being used outside the country and require foreign currencies to be handed over to the central bank. This prevents Icelanders from freely engaging in international trade. The creator(s) stated on Auroracoin's website that "The people of Iceland are being sacrificed at the altar of a flawed financial system," and that "The power must be taken away from the politicians and given back to the people. Cryptocurrencies are a very important milestone in this fight for liberty." However, Auroracoin may still have some legal hurdles. Iceland's central bank has taken notice of cryptocurrencies, especially Bitcoin and Auroracoin, and has already declared that buying bitcoins from foreign entities and using bitcoins (and presumably other cryptocurrencies) to bypass capital controls would be illegal.

Regardless, Auroracoin started out strong, but its value remains highly volatile because of the airdrop. Its peak price was USD 5.40, but it fell to around $3 later on. Many predict the price will continue to fall as more Icelanders claim their free coins, but the future price of Auroracoin is truly uncertain.

While it is uncertain whether Auroracoin will be a success or not, it is not the first cryptocurrency of its kind, and many other cryptocurrencies are being created for other nations as well. The same concept is behind Mazacoin, which was intended to be the official currency in the traditional Lakota Nation. Like Auroracoin, it is intended to help the tribe's economy but is also intended to increase the tribe's sovereignty. Mazacoin is still awaiting confirmation on whether it is truly the tribe's official currency.

Other national-based cryptocurrencies have also sprung up in the wake of Auroracoin, also with similar goals. Scotcoin and Spaincoin, currencies for Scotland and Spain respectively, were created in the wake of Auroracoin with the intent to help the nations' respective economies and also have a distribution system similar to Auroracoin. Only time will tell if nation-based coins are the future for cryptocurrencies.

Primecoin

Primecoin (XMP) was launched in 2013. The main innovation introduced by Primecoin is that its proof-of-work function produces somewhat useful scientific results. This contrasts with most proof-of-work functions, such as SHA256 or scrypt, whose results do not have any value except to secure the blockchain. Primecoin's proof-of-work function searches for chains of prime numbers, known as Cunningham chains. The chains of primes found through the proof-of-work could help researchers understand the distribution of prime numbers, which in turn could lead to advances in other scientific disciplines such as physics, or could have useful applications still unknown.

Practical proof-of-work functions must have two properties:

They must be effectively verifiable. Verification must be computationally fast. Many scientific computations are not easily verifiable. One example is folding@home, whose goal is to solve the problem of protein folding. The problem with using protein folding as a proof-of-work is that there is no fast way to verify that a given result (the shape of the folded protein) is correct. Thus miners would have an incentive to present fake results to collect the mining reward. The only way to check the solution would be to run the whole folding algorithm again, which defeats the purpose of a proof-of-work function.

The difficulty must be easily adjustable. The proof-of-work difficulty should be easy to adjust gradually in reaction to new miners entering or exiting the network.

The SHA256 hash function meets both properties, but it has been notoriously difficult to find scientific problems which can be adapted to these properties. Primecoin is the first proposal of a scientific problem that meets both requirements. Verification of a (relatively small) prime number is efficient on current hardware. Verification of chains of primes is similarly efficient. The length of the prime chains is used to adjust the difficulty. The only problem is that the length of a prime chain is a discrete value whose difficulty increases exponentially. Primecoin developers solved this problem, using a fractional chain length.

Primecoin targets a block generation period of one minute, with a difficult adjustment after every block. The block reward is not a fixed number of coins, as in Bitcoin, but it is a function of the difficulty: blockreward = 999/difficulty2. It can be shown that this self-adjusting block reward will lead to a fixed monetary supply.

Primecoin could be a first step towards creating proof-of-work functions that would solve useful problems.

Freicoin

Freicoin (FRC), launched in 2012, is an alt-coin based on Bitcoin with the main differentiator that it has demurrage. Demurrage is implemented as a tax on transactions that levies a certain fraction of the freicoins. This fraction increases with the time elapsed since the freicoins were last transacted. Thus demurrage acts as a negative interest rate on currency holders. Freicoin applies an annual demurrage fee of approximately 5%, depending on certain operations in the network. The name Freicoin is a tribute to the monetary system Freigeld proposed by Silvio Gesell.

According to its proponents, demurrage serves two purposes:

It creates an economic incentive to invest. In this sense, demurrage is similar to expansionary monetary policies that increase the money supply and thus create inflation. The advantage of demurrage over inflation is that the demurrage effect is constant and thus it is easier to account for6.

It allows miners to be compensated indefinitely through block rewards without creating an inflationary monetary base because the block reward will be paid with the demurrage fee. This might be an advantage over cryptocurrencies that rely on transaction fees substituting block rewards on the medium term.

Demurrage disincentives hoarding of freicoins, as the coins will lose value quickly. This contrasts with the estimations that a large percentage of bitcoins have never been involved in any transaction, presumably because they are being hoarded. On the other hand, critics argue that this could limit its growth. Later versions of Freicoin plan to implement digital assets and contracts.

Other Alt-Coins

This section presents a quick assortment of other alt-coins in no particular order, stressing the singular features of each:

SolarCoin aims to incentivize solar energy. SolarCoin uses two mining algorithms: a regular proof-of-work algorithm, and a second one that relies on a verified energy meter reading. Producers of solar energy can submit their proof-of-generation and be granted SolarCoins.

Aphroditecoin replicates the concept of Auroracoin in Cyprus. Similarly, SpainCoin replicates the concept in Spain.

Splash is a fork of Ripple where the native currency is mined.

Anoncoin is a fork of Bitcoin that works over the Invisible Internet Project (I2P), an anonymizing network.

DarkCoin is a fork of Bitcoin that incorporates technology for sending transactions with increased privacy for its users .

CryptoNote is an open source project that allows the creation of cryptocurrencies. Its innovation is that it uses ring signatures7, instead of ECDSA signatures, for decreased traceability.

TAGCoin is positioned as a reward system for merchants. Merchants can buy tag-coins and give them to their customers, who can then use the tagcoins with other merchants or cash them in.

Devcoin, whose purpose is to support open source developers.

Safecoin, whose purpose is to fund the SAFE network, proposed by Maidsafe. SAFE is a peer-to-peer network where users contribute computational power and storage to a public cloud, where data can be stored securely in a decentralized way.

CureCoin whose goal is to reward scientific/medicinal research, such as protein folding computations.

Qixcoin is a cryptocurrency whose purpose is to support peer-to-peer gaming, both strategy, and chance games. It has a built-in engine to verify card games.

NEM

NEO

XEM

ZCash

QTUM etc.

The Case For/Against Alt-Coins

The cost of launching an alt-coin is very low:
just forking the Bitcoin Core source code
and changing the logo is enough to create
an alt-coin. For this reason, the number of
alt-coins launched is very large. Many of the
first alt-coins introduced few changes to
Bitcoin's implementation, and critics argue
that their main goal was to replicate the
scarcity race of Bitcoin.

Critics of alt-coins argue that only alt-coins
that have some feature impossible to add
to Bitcoin and that fulfill some unmet need
will survive. Otherwise, Bitcoin will capture
a dominant market share because of the
network effect. The network effect, or
network externalities, refers to the property
of a product or a technology whose demand
increases with the number of users. The
classic example of a product with network
effect is the telephone, which is more
useful the more people are connected to

the network. These are direct network effects. Another classical example is the DVD standard, where the more users that have a DVD player, the more attractive it is for content producers to support the platform. These are indirect network effects. Bitcoin advocates argue that Bitcoin exhibits both direct network effects (the more people use Bitcoin as a store of value, the more value it has) and indirect network effects (the more people would like to spend Bitcoin, the greater the incentive of merchants to support it).

Liquidity is the economic manifestation of the network effect. The liquidity of an asset is the degree to which it can be sold quickly without affecting its price. Liquidity is a measure of the trade-off between the speed of the sale and the price drop. The liquidity of a currency depends on the size of the network of users of that currency. Critics of alt-coins argue that liquidity is self-reinforcing, and thus users will gravitate towards the most liquid cryptocurrency, making it even more liquid. This process, they argue, will drive alt-coins to extinction.

On the other hand, proponents of alt-coins argue that the network effect does not necessarily happen on a global scale, and there can be room for network effects to kick in along, say, national borders or language divide. Furthermore, there might be room for complementary technologies to Bitcoin, even with the network effect taking place.

Aside from network effects, other economic arguments criticizing alt-coins are:

Competing standards do not make sense for currencies. A single standard increases the value to all users. Thus competing standards serve no purpose, and currency competition can lead to fragmentation.

Switching costs. There can be significant switching costs from Bitcoin to alt-coin once much of the payment infrastructure is laid out. Defendants of alt-coins argue that switching can be done via a software upgrade in most cases and that several cryptocurrencies can easily co-exist thanks to tools such as multi-currency wallets and exchanges that automatically integrate with such wallets.

Coordination problems. Even if most users would like to substitute Bitcoin for an alt-coin—say because of a technological advantage—they suffer from a coordination problem that makes the transition difficult.

Arguments often put forward in favor of alt-coins are:

Competition is good because it leads to innovation. However, critics of alt-coins respond that there is already a lot of innovation in the Bitcoin community, and this internal innovation is more important that innovating the basic technology. Furthermore, technical innovation is already happening using Bitcoin as a layer, such as in several meta-coins projects. Proponents of alt-coins argue back that it is very risky to include new technology into Bitcoin (or in some cases, it cannot be technically included) and that innovating by creating a new alt-coin is a much safer option. Moreover, alt-coins enable permissionless innovation, that is, they allow trying ideas that would be vetted by Bitcoin developers. Critics reply that innovation on the features of digital currencies can be achieved without diluting the monetary base of Bitcoin using side-chains.

<u>Multiple blockchains can help reduce the load on the network.</u> If at some point Bitcoin encounters dis-economies of scale, such as blockchain scalability troubles, alt-coins could be of an advantage as they would allow reducing the load on the

Bitcoin network. Critics of alt-coins reply that if another blockchain is needed for some functionality, then nodes will have to support the new alt-coin blockchain and the original Bitcoin blockchain. Moreover, as there might be transactions between the two, the overall burden on the nodes will be greater.

Some alt-coins can help achieve a public function. One example is alt-coins whose proof-of-work achieves a useful scientific goal such as Primecoin. Another example is alt-coins created to fund public goods, such as Devcoin, CureCoin, or Safecoin. Similarly, branded alt-coins can be created to fund artists or other projects.

Alt-coins can help lower Bitcoin's volatility, by putting a cap on its market capitalization.

Some alt-coins do not need to compete directly with Bitcoin but might cooperate in a mutually beneficial relationship. One example could be an alt-coin that allows for very low transaction costs—say to use in micro payments—and <u>could reduce Bitcoin's scalability pressures.</u>

Critics of alt-currencies also cite practical disadvantages to the development of alt-coins:

Alt-coins are a way to get around Bitcoin's fixed money supply. Critics argue that the main objective of most alt-coins is to create a scarcity race that tries to mimic the scarcity race carried out by Bitcoin, with the objective of enriching their creators. The result is that with many alt-coins the money supply just becomes infinite.

Alt-coins divert talent. Time and effort spent developing and promoting alt-coins could be used instead to advance Bitcoin's technology and marketing message.

They confuse potential users, who would have to learn the differences between many cryptocurrencies before deciding to use any of them.

If an alt-coin were to supersede Bitcoin, this would open the door for yet another alt-coin to supersede it and so on. Eventually, users would hesitate to give significant value to any cryptocurrency because of fear that it would get supplanted by the next one.

A tally on the rivalry between different cryptocurrencies can be taken by comparing their market capitalizations.

Bitcoin and several alt-coins have been competing for some years now. As of the time of writing, it seems Bitcoin has been able to benefit from the first-mover advantage, enabled by network effects and liquidity, and capture a significant portion of the crypto-currencies' market. Time will tell whether this advantage will extend over time or whether some alt-coin or meta-coin could challenge Bitcoin.

Bitcoin Vs. Goldcoin

Bitcoin... Monetary Nirvana?

Naturally, proponents of Bitcoin, those who benefit from the growth of Bitcoin, insist rather loudly that 'for sure, Bitcoin is money' and not only that but 'it is the best money ever, the money of the future,' etc. Well, the proponents of Fiat shout just as loudly that paper currency is money and we all know that Fiat paper is not money by any means, as it lacks the most important attributes of real money. The question then is does Bitcoin even qualify as money, never mind it being the money of the future or the best money ever.

To find out, let's look at the attributes that define money, and see if Bitcoin qualifies. The three essential attributes of money are;

1. To find out, let's look at the attributes that define money, and see if Bitcoin

qualifies. The three essential attributes of money are;

2. money is the numeraire, the unit of account.

3. money is a medium of exchange, but other things can also fulfill this function, i.e., direct barter, the 'netting out' of goods exchanged. Also 'trade goods' that hold value temporarily; and finally the exchange of mutual credit; i.e., netting out the value of promises fulfilled by exchanging bills or IOU's.

Compared to Fiat, Bitcoin does not do too badly as a medium of exchange. Fiat is only accepted in the geographic domain of its issuer. Dollars are no good in Europe etc. Bitcoin is accepted internationally. On the other hand, very few retailers currently accept payment in Bitcoin. Unless the acceptance grows geometrically, Fiat wins; although at the cost of exchange between countries.

The first condition is a lot tougher; money must be a stable store of value. Now Bitcoins have gone from a 'value' of $3.00 to around $17,000+, in just a few years. This is about as far from being a 'stable store of value'; as you can get! Indeed, such gains are a perfect example of a speculative boom like Dutch tulip bulbs, or junior mining companies, or Nortel stocks.

Of course, Fiat fails here as well; for example, the US Dollar, the 'main' Fiat, has lost over 95% of its value in a few decades... neither fiat nor Bitcoin qualify in the most important measure of money; the capacity to store value and preserve value through time. Real money that is Gold has shown the ability to hold value not just for centuries, but for eons. Neither Fiat nor Bitcoin has this crucial capacity... **both fail as money.**

Finally, we come to the second attribute; that of being the numeraire. Now, this is interesting, and we can see why both Bitcoin and Fiat fail as money, by looking closely at the question of the 'numeraire.' Numeraire refers to the use of money to not only store value, but to in a sensed measure, or compare value. In Austrian economics, it is considered impossible actually to measure value; after all, value resides only in human consciousness and how can anything in consciousness be measured? Nevertheless, through the principle of Mengerian market action, that is an interaction between bid and offer, market prices can be established, if only momentarily and this market price is expressed regarding the numeraire, the most marketable good, that is money.

So how do we establish the value of Fiat? Through the concept of 'purchasing power' that is, the value of Fiat is determined by what it can be traded for... a so called 'basket of goods.' But this implies that Fiat has no value of its own, rather value flows from the value of the goods and services it may be traded for. Causality flows from the goods 'bought' to the Fiat number. After all, what difference is there between a one Dollar bill and a hundred Dollar bill, except the number printed on it and the purchasing power of the number?

Gold, on the other hand, is not measured by what it trades for; rather, uniquely, it is measured by another physical standard; by its weight or mass. A gram of Gold is a gram of gold, and an ounce of Gold is an ounce of Gold... no matter what number is engraved on its surface, 'face value' or otherwise. Causality is opposite to that of Fiat; Gold is measured by weight, an intrinsic quality not by purchasing power. Now, have you any idea of the value of an ounce of Dollars? No such thing. Fiat is only 'measured' by an ephemeral quantity... the number printed on it, the 'face value.'

Bitcoin is farther away from being the numeraire; not only is it simply a number, much as Fiat, but its value is measured in Fiat! Even if Bitcoin becomes internationally accepted as a medium of exchange, and even if it manages to replace the Dollar as the accepted 'numeraire,' it can never have an intrinsic measure as Gold has. Gold is unique in being measured by a true, unchanging physical quantity. Gold is unique in storing value for thousands of years. Nothing else in reach of humanity has this unique combination of qualities.

In conclusion, while Bitcoin has some advantages over Fiat, namely anonymity, and decentralization, it fails in its claim to being money. Its advantages are also questionable; the intent is to limit the 'mining' of Bitcoins to 26,000,000 units; that is, the 'mining' algorithm gets harder and harder to solve, then impossible after the 26 million Bitcoins are mined. Unfortunately, this announcement could very well be the death knell of Bitcoin; already, some central banks have announced that Bitcoins may become a 'reservable' currency.

Wow, sounds like a major step for Bitcoin, does it not? After all, the 'big banks' seem to be accepting the true value of the Bitcoin, no? What this means is banks recognize that they could trade Fiat for Bitcoins and to buy up the 26 million Bitcoins planned would cost a meager 26 Billion Fiat Dollars. Twenty-six billion Dollars is not even small change to the Fiat printers; it is about a week's worth of printing by the US Fed alone. And, once the Bitcoins bought up and locked up in the Fed's 'wallet'... what useful purpose could they serve?

There would be no Bitcoins left in circulation; a perfect corner. If there are no Bitcoins in circulation, how on Earth could they be used as a medium of exchange?

And, what could the issuers of Bitcoin possibly do to defend against such a fate? Change the algorithm and increase the 26 million to... 52 million? To 104 million? Join the Fiat printing parade? But then, by the quantity theory of money, Bitcoin would start to lose value, just as Fiat supposedly loses value through 'overprinting.'

We come to the key Issue; why search for a 'new money' when we already have the very best money, Gold? Fear of Gold confiscation? Lack of anonymity from an intrusive government? Brutal taxation? Fiat money legal tender laws? All of the above. The answer is not in a new form of money, but in a new social structure, one without Fiat, without Government spying, without drones and swat teams without IRS, border guards, TSA thugs... on and on. A world of liberty, not tyranny. Once this is accomplished, Gold will resume its ancient and vital role as honest money and not a moment before.

PRESENT AND FUTURE OPPORTUNITIES

Consumer Acceptance And Potential Growth

Cryptocurrency growth over the next year is expected to be solid but not spectacular, and it is important to note that this growth starts from a very low base. The frequency of use is expected to remain low.

A consumer survey showed that, of those who have used cryptocurrencies within the last five years, only 17% are "very" or "extremely" concerned about cryptocurrencies. Almost half (48%) say they are only "slightly" concerned for any reason, and 12% say they are not at all concerned. When asked about their concerns, cryptocurrency users cite fraud, followed by fluctuations in value, and acceptance among vendors. These concerns are real and represent significant hurdles that must be addressed before cryptocurrency is widely accepted.

Respondents are bullish about cryptocurrencies' potential impact on banking and retail. A majority (76%) of current users say cryptocurrencies will redefine banking as we know it, and 59% say their banking experience would be improved if they had greater access to cryptocurrencies.

Striking The Right Balance

In the short term, businesses will find success if they can strike the right balance between growing market demand and an evolving regulatory landscape. For example, strategic partnerships formed by companies such as Coinbase and BitPay serve as bitcoin "wallets" and payment processors for merchants. By holding the digital wallets that receive bitcoin payments from customers, and then immediately paying those merchants the cash value of those bitcoins, Coinbase and BitPay effectively enable merchants to accept cryptocurrency payments without taking on the risks of holding bitcoins on their books. Forging these types of strategic partnerships and solutions is the key to driving the market forward in the short term.

As the regulatory landscape develops and the market matures, more traditional business strategies may begin to play a greater role in achieving success. However, as with most groundbreaking markets, the combination of ingenuity and speed to market is likely to distinguish the market leaders.

Emerging Markets

Perhaps the greatest opportunity for those involved in the cryptocurrency ecosystem is at the potential this technology has in developing economies. In fact, rapidly developing technology has enabled many emerging economies to skip entire stages of development completely. For example, cell phones made it unnecessary for African countries to build telephone lines. Similarly, cryptocurrency may one day enable developing economies to forgo the need to build large financial infrastructures, clearing houses, and other third-party intermediaries.

There is already strong evidence of this concept at work in the M-Pesa and M-Paisa systems that have developed in Kenya and India, respectively. Cryptocurrency will likely build on these innovations to offer the potential for micro payments and cheaper remittances across borders. If cryptocurrency can offer lower cost solutions for economically disadvantaged populations, this may be the technology's greatest legacy.

What This Means for Your Business

The cryptocurrency market is still in its infancy. Robust growth may take root first in international markets rather than in the United States, where a strong financial system makes the need for a currency revolution less than obvious. Our survey reinforces the idea that cryptocurrencies as a whole remain a niche product, but key indicators—consumers' expectations that their use of cryptocurrency will increase and the growing use of digital wallets—point to a consumer base that is open to change.

There are challenges for cryptocurrency in the near term. With so many of its characteristics falling between currency, a financial asset, and a technology protocol, the pace of growth and adoption may splinter the industry. This could happen as various participants seek their way to derive value from the concept of cryptocurrency. As a disruptive technology, it will continue to divide opinion and face skepticism. As regulatory standards are adopted and refined, creative products enter the market, and the prices of the various cryptocurrencies stabilize, we'll see greater confidence on the part of all market participants.

This confidence and trust will need to be nurtured by the industry itself, using the guidance of trusted advisors to bridge the gaps between this new technology, the established principles that govern it, and the market demands that drive it.

If the pace of growth continues at a steady pace, it may not be long before the next iteration of cryptocurrency offers new ways of transfer, as well as wealth and asset creation that may reshape much of what we previously thought was possible on the Internet.

In our view, however, the more important potential disruptor is the blockchain public ledger technology that underlies cryptocurrency. This technology has the potential to open the door to revolutionary possibilities in multiple industries. Escrow accounts, securities and financial instrument offerings, "smart contracts," and electoral systems are just a few of the concepts that are being discussed. Any financial asset that currently requires a trusted third party to provide verification could, theoretically, be disrupted.

Could Bitcoin Change the Game in Africa?

Despite slow progress so far, some see digital currency as the next step in helping many Africans enter the formal economy

In the wildest of claims, Bitcoin – the virtual paperless and stateless currency transacted on the borderless internet – was going to tear apart traditional money transfer companies and help alleviate poverty.

Accessing the multi-billion-dollar remittance flows to Africa certainly has substantial appeal, perhaps helping to attract some large seed investments in African bitcoin start-ups.

Firms have also sought to draw users to bitcoin by undercutting the high costs of international money transfers. Some of its backers even claim it could leapfrog traditional financial infrastructure on a continent where two-thirds of people are "unbanked."

Parts of Africa have already come a long way in developing mobile money payment systems that give the unbanked millions a chance to move into the formal economy. Advocates of Bitcoin on the continent say it would take this a step further, though it requires an internet connection which more than three-quarters of Africans still do not have.

A small group of users – mainly in South Africa, Kenya and Nigeria – trade speculatively in bitcoin via online forex sites, as they would any other asset.

Africa hosts several established bitcoin exchange services, such as ICE3X and BitX in South Africa and BitPesa in several countries in east and west Africa, where users can trade between bitcoin and traditional currencies. Peer-to-peer trading sites such as LocalBitcoins.com are also popular – in early June, nearly KES10m was traded via the site in Kenya in one week.

"You don't need a third party – in Kenya, you can send money via M-Pesa direct to my phone in exchange for the bitcoins you buy. There has been an amazing increase in volumes traded," said Michael Kimani, head of the African Digital Currency Association.

One of the biggest opportunities for bitcoin could be online payments, but I've also seen people funding online wallets, using it for online sports betting.

Spending bitcoin in the region is more difficult. South Africa's largest online marketplace, Bidorbuy, introduced bitcoin payments on its site; a handful of other online retailers, mostly in South Africa, already accept the digital currency. In most cases, a bitcoin exchange company handles the back-end of the transaction, while merchants quote prices in local currency.

Despite slow progress so far, Nii Quaynor, often described as the "father of the internet in Africa," told the Guardian that "digital currency and transaction frameworks for the internet are the next step" for the continent. In March, the company he chairs, Ghana Dot Com (GDC), launched what it claims is Africa's first bitcoin mining facility.

Quaynor is hopeful too about the potential for blockchain technology – the distributed transaction ledger seen as the cornerstone of bitcoin innovation – and says non-financial applications around land registries and voting could be transformative. Banks in Africa are also looking into potential uses of the blockchain.

Bitcoin still exists in a very niche space. There was early excitement about virtual currency – especially as an affordable way for Africans in the diaspora to send money home – but this has subsided as a result of price volatility, nervousness around anonymity and security, and difficulties understanding the product. As there are increases in bitcoin adoption, governments, and central banks are considering regulating the sector, which some users think will legitimise bitcoin and others fear might make it more difficult to transact.

For now, though, Africa's bitcoin fans are set to keep on trading.

Should I invest In It?

Bitcoin has grown strongly but with plenty of volatility along the way. Over the past 12 months, its price has risen from $1220 to $1775, according to figures from coinmarketcap.com. It has also shown resilience, with the price rallying after the Bitfinex hack and bitconnect closeup. In short, this is not a haven: despite excitable claims, the price could hit $20,000, where it goes next is anybody's guess, so investors should approach with caution.

Lex Deak, chief executive of alternative investment aggregator Off3r, says investing in Bitcoin isn't for the fainthearted. "You should only invest a small proportion of your money and be prepared for massive swings in value."

The early gold rush days are over, he adds, and buyers shouldn't treat it as a get-rich-quick scheme. "You could double your money within a year, but you could easily lose it all," he says.

Marc Warne, the founder of Bittylicious, a site where bitcoins can be bought, says novice investors should start modestly. "Just buy a small amount, to begin with, say £30, to learn how it works, how to trade it, and how to handle it safely in a wallet," he says. He advises against investing large sums unless you understand crypto currencies and computer security.

As bitcoin has a finite supply, future price movement will depend on demand, Warne says. "Bitcoin will be used more in the future because it's the first time that something not fully controlled by any entity like a government or bank has been used over the internet. It has been around for about nine years now without any fundamental issues."

Is it Safe?

Bitcoin cannot be hacked, manipulated or altered, but exchanges or digital wallets are vulnerable, just like online bank accounts, Warne says. "If you hold bitcoin in any form you instantly become a target," he adds.

Since bitcoin doesn't exist, what is stored in the wallet are the secure digital keys used to access specific details of the bitcoin. The private key is a secret code which allows the user to prove ownership of their bitcoin. Wallets can be installed on smartphones using an app, or currency exchanges can run web-based wallets. Buyers need to make sure their computer's security is up to scratch, and must also trust the exchange, which needs high-level security to prevent hacking.

James Hill, the software developer at consultancy Scott Logic, says the core blockchain algorithm, which underpins all cryptocurrencies, remains secure. He says the real danger comes from losing the keys that prove buyers own their coins.

If you are hacked, there is no way of claiming a refund from a bank or regulatory authority because none exists.

Word of Warning

As with all technology, something better may one day come along. When that happens, bitcoin's value could collapse to near-zero, probably in a matter of hours or minutes, in a spectacular ball of flames. It has no support structure to prop it up as a normal currency does. Do not treat this as a long-term store of value to fund your retirement.

It will remain a fringe investment until it is officially recognized and regulated.

Ordinary currency investing is risky enough, but bitcoin is even riskier.

Binary Options Bitcoin Trading Platform

Binary options brokers are getting familiar with the popularity of these Bitcoins, and its constant fluctuating values. Therefore they are using this opportunity to offer traders with the latest volatile crypto-currency as an additional payment method. Bitcoin brokers providing crypto-currency as trading option include -

One touch option - Bitcoin trading can be done with AnyOption or one-touch option. For example, the popular currency pair is BTC/USD.

SetOption - The option available for asset trading is BITCOIN/USD.

Bitcoin brokers provide a simple trading online platform. All you have to do is visit their website, enter your details, and create an account. You can start with a demo account to understand the market action.

TIPS FOR TRADING BITCOIN AND ALTCOINS

Safety rules were written with blood. That statement sounds familiar to every soldier around. Although we are not dealing with a risk to human lives, losing your expensive Bitcoins by making mistakes trading is definitely not a fun situation.

So, how we can avoid those mistakes in our trading? How to be mostly on the green side? First, it is important to note that to trade right requires attention and your one hundred percent focus. Secondly, trading is not for everyone. The following tips are easy to internalize because these tips were "written in blood." However, it's still difficult to apply them in real-time. After all, we are not rational human beings.

Have a reason before entering each trade: Start a trade only when you know why you're starting and have a clear strategy for afterwards.

Not all traders make gains from trading, since this is a zero-sum game (for everyone who benefits someone else loses on the other side).The Altcoins market is driven by large whales (yes, the same ones responsible for placing huge blocks of hundreds of Bitcoins on the order book). The whales are just waiting patiently for innocent little fish to make mistakes. Even if you aspire to trade on a daily basis, sometimes it is better not to earn and do nothing, instead of jumping into the rushing water and exposing your coins to losses. From my experience, there are days where you only keep your profits by not trading at all.

Target and stop when starting a trade: For each trade we must set a clear target level for taking profit and more importantly, a stop-loss level for cutting losses. A Stop-loss is setting the level of loss where the trade will get closed.

Here again, it is important considering a number of factors when choosing a stop loss level correctly. Most traders fail when they fall in love with a trade or the coin itself. They may say, "Here it will turn around, and I will get out of this trade with a minimum loss, I'm sure". They're letting their ego take control of them and unlike the traditional stock exchange where extreme daily movements are considered 2-3% in value, Crypto trades are a lot more riskier: in my life as a trader I've seen a coin dumping by 80% just in a few hours! And nobody wants to be the one who is left holding it.

Meet FOMO (fear of missing out): Indeed, it really isn't fun to see such situations from the outside – when a certain coin is being pumped up like crazy with huge two-digit gains in minutes.

That bold green candle yells at you "you are the only one not holding me". At exactly this point you will notice lame people flooding the Crypto forums and the exchanges' Troll boxes to talk about this pump. But what do we do now? Very simple, Keep moving forward. True, it's possible that many may have caught the rise ahead of us and it can continue raising, but bare in mind that the whales are just waiting for small buyers on the way up to sell them the coins they bought in cheaper prices. Prices are now high and it's clear that the current coin holders only consist of those little fish. Needless to say, the next step is usually the bright red candle which sells through the whole order book.

Risk Management: little pig eats a lot, big pig gets eaten. This statement tells the story of the market profits from our perspective. To be a profitable trader, you never look for the peak of the movement. You look for the small profits that will accumulate into a big one.

Manage risk wisely across your portfolio. For example, you should never invest more than small percentage of your portfolio in a non-liquid market (very high risk). To those trades we will assign greater tolerance – the stop and target levels will be chosen far from the buying level.

The underlying asset creates volatile market conditions: Most Altcoins are traded according to the Bitcoin value.

Bitcoin is a volatile asset (relative to FIAT) and this fact should be taken into consideration, especially in the days when the Bitcoin value is moving sharply. Bitcoin and Altcoins have an inverse relationship in their value, i.e. when the value of Bitcoin rises then Altcoins are losing their Bitcoin value, and vice versa. When Bitcoin is volatile, our conditions for trading are kind of foggy. During fog we can't see much ahead, so it is better to have close targets for our trades or not to trade at all.

Most Altcoins lose their value over time. They simply bleed their value away slowly (sometimes rapidly).

Take this into account when holding Alts for the medium and long term, and of course choose them carefully. What kind of Alts are recommended for the long term? Remember, this is only when there is a reason for making a trade. The projects/coins that have a higher daily trading volume and which have a widespread community behind them, with continuous development, are here to stay with us:

Ethereum ETH, Monero XMR, Factom FCT, DASH, are all leading coins and traded the most volume daily. You should follow the coin's chart and identify low and stable periods. Such periods are likely to be a consolidation period by the whales, and when the right time comes, accompanied by a good press release of the project, the pump will start and they will sell in profit.

A word about public ICOs (crowd-sales): Many new projects choose to make a crowd-sale where they offer investors an early opportunity to buy a share of the project (tokens or coins) in what is meant to be a good price for the tokens.

The motivation for the investors is that the token will be traded from day one on the exchanges and would yield a nice profit to the ICO participants. In recent years, there have been many successful ICOs, both the project itself and especially in measuring the yield for investors. Coins doubled, or tripled, their value and much more in relation to their value on the crowd sale. Augur's preliminary crowd-sale yielded investors a phenomenal 1,000% for their investment. Okay, but what's the catch here? Not all the projects benefit their investors. Many ICOs proved to be complete scams, not only were they not being traded at all but some projects disappeared with the money and we have not heard from them right up to this day.

So how do you know if you should invest in an ICO? It's not about science, it is important to pay attention to the level of seriousness of the project and its team. Look for the project's website (does it look like a child has built it during computer school?), Who is the team behind the project – Are they hiding behind nicknames or proudly present themselves on their website? Pay attention to the Bitcointalk thread (does it exist at all?) and how the team members respond to technical questions. Is there a large community behind the project? Expect to see a Slack gathering its community. Watch out the amount raised: A project which had raised too little will probably not be able to develop over time, a project which had raised huge amount – there won't be enough investors left out there to buy coins on exchanges. And most importantly is risk management. Never put all eggs in one basket and invest too much of your portfolio in one ICO.

A final tip – practical steps to implement right away:

❖ Fees, fees, fees: Multiple trade actions = More fees. It's always advisable to post the command (maker) and not to buy from the order book (taker). In Poloniex exchange, the difference is 0.1% in favor of the maker. That's quite a bit.

❖ Traders with no pressure: Don't start trading unless you have the optimal conditions to make the decision to start a trade and know when and how to get out of it. Pressure almost always creates losing trades. Wait for the next opportunity, you will get there.

❖ Setting goals and placing sell orders: always set your goals by putting sell orders. You don't know when a whale will pump your coin up to catch your command (and pay a reduced fee on the "maker" side, remember?).

A successful strategy regarding this is placing very low buy orders. Sometime ago, a crazy dump occurred, selling off Augor coin down to 25% of its value! After a short while the market recovered slightly and anyone who had low buy these low orders could easily double or triple their investment. Placing buy orders requires special care, don't wake up when you're far away from the market to find your buy order is suddenly higher than the current market price!

❖ Buy the rumor, sell the news. When major news sites publish articles it is usually exactly the right time to actually get out of the trade.

❖ You have made a good trade, but as always, the moment you sold your coin runs up again! First, meet this guy – Murphy's Law. Secondly, read over what was written on the news and never enter position again under pressure. As long as there is profit – you are ok. Go on to your next trade and don't find yourself losing it.

❖ Leave your ego aside. The goal here is not to be right on your trades, but to make a profit. Do not waste resources (time and money) to try to prove that you should've been entering that trade. Remember, there is no trader who never loses, at least sometimes. The equation is simple – get the total profits to be higher than the total losses.

Altcoin Flipping

The year of 2017 was definitely the year of crypto, especially that the market capital of cryptocurrencies reached its all time high according to data from coinmarketcap.com.

People have been flipping Altcoins. Some traded across many cryptocurrency exchanges including Poloniex, binance, yobit, Hitbtc, Bittrex and Cryptsy which ended by an exit scam by its owner Paul Vernon.

What is Altcoin Flipping?

Altcoin flipping refers to day trading of various altcoins. If you are flipping altcoins, then you are buying and selling them for bitcoin, rather than fiat currencies. Note that most altcoins can only be bought via bitcoin, not via fiat currencies. Only a handful of altcoins can be bought via fiat currencies including ethereum, monero, ripple, ethereum classic, dash and a few more.

Altcoin flipping is a form of cryptocurrency trading approach followed by many cryptocurrency traders and speculators.

When you trade altcoins for bitcoin, you can use cryptocurrency exchanges such as Poloniex.com, Hitbtc.com and Bittrex.com without having to pass through any verification processes to deposit or withdraw your bitcoin capital.

So, now as we know what altcoin flipping is, let us start:

Acquiring Bitcoin To Start Trading and Flipping Altcoins:

The great thing about altcoin flipping, and cryptocurrency trading in general, is that you can start trading with a small amount; even with $10-20 worth of bitcoin. So, you can either buy some bitcoin using a service like Paxful.com, which enables you to buy small amounts of bitcoin using credit cards, paypal money, western union, amazon gift cards and other payment methods, or earn some bitcoin through many ways that can help you acquire a small amount of bitcoin ($10-20) to start your altcoin flipping adventure. Here are a few examples of ways to earn some free bitcoin:

1. Mining Bytecoin using Minergate With Your PC:

Minergate is a cryptocurrency mining service that offers a simple software that can enable you to mine some altcoins using your PC. Go to Minergate's website, create an account, download and install the software. After installing the software, launch it. On the main interface of Minergate's client, click on the "Miner" button, where you will be prompted with a group of coins to choose which one you want to mine.

2. Bitcoin and Altcoin Faucets:

Faucets are websites that reward their visitors with small amounts of bitcoins or altcoins at regular intervals. Faucet owners profit from this business model via advertising, especially that faucets attract a large number of visitors who come for some free money! You can find hundreds, if not thousands, of cryptocurrency faucets by just using Google, but pay attention to two important things:

1. Always use faucets that have good reviews that prove they really pay their visitors.
2. Some faucets can contain malware and some annoying pop-up adds. I would not recommend using such faucets.

I will only present you with two reliable faucets that really pay their visitors to start with: Moonbitcoin and Moondogecoin , but do your research, you will surely find many others. If you spend 3-4 hours browsing faucets, you can accumulate around $1 worth of crypto.

3. Bitcoin Paid-to-Click (PTC) Sites:

PTC sites are a group of sites that reward their users for viewing ads. There are currently many websites that offer bitcoin PTC ads, but as we mentioned in faucets, always do your research before using any PTC service to make sure you will actually be paid for your time and effort.

BTCClicks is a reliable PTC service that pays you for viewing ads in bitcoin. You can find many other similar sites by searching through bitcointalk.org and talkgold.com

Creating Accounts on Cryptocurrency Exchanges:

It is advised to use more than one cryptocurrency exchange. For the purpose of this book, we will use three exchanges; Poloniex, Hitbtc and Bittrex. Note the following:

1. Create an account on an exchange. Create a strong password for each account. Don't use words or phrases, instead use a randomly generated password. I recommend using an online password generator like passwordsgenerator.net to create a

random password of a minimum of 16 characters.

2. Use two-factor authentication to maximize the security of your accounts.

3. Some coins are only available for trading on an exchange, but not the other, so you will need to use them all in special conditions, but I recommend using Poloniex for most of your altcoin flipping trades.

Depositing Your Bitcoin To Your Exchange's Wallet:

To start trading, you will have to deposit your bitcoin to the exchange's wallet. I am going to show you how to deposit your bitcoin to your wallet on Poloniex:

1. On your Poloniex account page, press Balances -> Deposits and Withdrawals, on the top right part of your main account page.

2. You will be prompted with a page that includes a list of all coins available on the exchange's platform. Beside "bitcoin", click on the "Deposit" link, your wallet's deposit address will appear

3. Use this address to send your bitcoins. Note that your coins will not be added to your wallet on Poloniex, except after the transaction has received three confirmations. Sometimes, the deposit takes a long time to appear on your account, around 6-8 hours in some cases, so don't worry if this happens to you; the coins will eventually be added to your account.

Placing Buying Orders:

To start trading crypto on Poloniex, after your bitcoin deposit has been added successfully to your account, click on the "Exchange" button on the top left corner of your account's home page. Your will be prompted with a list of all available coins for trading. Note that on Poloniex, there are 4 markets; the bitcoin, ethereum, monero and USD markets. For altcoin flipping, you will only use the bitcoin trading market.

Now, let me show you how to buy your first altcoins:

I will show you how to buy some synero (AMP). So, on the list of coins available on the right side of the page, click on the synero (AMP) market.

__Note__: there are 2 buy order types: ordinary buy order and stop-limit buy order. We will buy synero using an ordinary buy order.

Use the box on the left hand-side which is titled "Buy AMP". You have to fill 2 box fields and the third field will be filled automatically for you. You have first to specify the price at which you want to buy your coins and then you can choose whether to specify the amount of synero you want to buy, or the amount of bitcoin you wish to spend buying synero.

Setting Sell Orders for Your Bought Coins:

After buying your coins, I recommend including them in a sell order as soon as possible, to make sure that your coins will be sold for profit, once your target price has been reached. Now, let me include the synero coins we have just bought into a sell order.

Determine your target price for selling your coins. For doing so, we will have to examine the AMPBTC chart. So, click on the 15 minutes candlesticks and then click on the 1 week button to look through synero's price during the past week,

By examining the charts, you will notice that synero's price has been following a pattern characterized by bullish bursts followed by downwards/upwards price correction attempts. The Fibonacci retracement level, which corresponds to BTC, is a good price target to aim at, especially if that level has been reached 3 times during the past week.

Setting up your sell order: Now, let's set up the sell order. Use the box on the right hand-side marked "Sell AMP". Enter the target price (BTC) and the full amount of coins bought, after subtracting the amount of commission charged by the exchange for the trade. The total amount of bitcoin is automatically calculated and added in the "Total" box. After setting the amount and price, you will have to press "Sell" to submit your sell order.

After successfully putting your "Sell order", you will be able to see it under "My open orders."

Whenever the target price is reached, your coins will be sold automatically, provided that there is enough sell orders.

Important Trading Tips:

As you will be flipping altcoins, try to enter trades that would last for a few days, better less than one week. The following are some important tips that would help you make some good profits:

1. Follow the golden rule of "Buy low, sell high". Look for coins that have repeated patterns, or coins that repeatedly swing between certain price levels. There are a lot of coins that behave this way.

2. Follow the charts to detect bullish waves and try to scalp them, i.e. find good entry points to buy and sell repeatedly as price goes up. For example, synero was following a bullish wave during an 8 weeks period and I found good entry points to buy, then sell repeatedly which helped me make some good profits.

3. Coins with high trading volumes, especially on Poloniex, can be very profitable. Usually, the first 2-3 days following the opening of a new altcoin market on an exchange will usually witness great price increases, so some good amount of money can be made.

4. Don't put all your eggs in one basket. I recommend dividing your capital, regardless how big it is, into 3-5 parts and use each part to buy one altcoin.

5. Look for price variations of the same coin on Poloniex, Hitbtc and Bittrex. Sometimes, you can buy it low on one exchange to sell it high on another.

WHAT IS A BITCOIN WHALE?

The term "whale" is frequently used to describe the big money Bitcoin players that show their hand in the Bitcoin market. The ocean as a metaphor for the market is apt, since one can then extend it to include the big fish and the small fish; sharks; rallies as feeding frenzies; waves as market moves; and so forth. It may be, however, that the term "whale" has been applied to the wrong class of investor because the players described next are truly the biggest creatures in the ocean.

Bitcoin Dolphins

They show themselves in the exchanges with orders of 1000 BTC, every now and again, and the common perception seems to be that the orderbook "whales" are the heavyweight players who move the market and can manipulate price if they so desire. However, this view is inaccurate.

The fact is that there are even bigger players than the so-called whales, who do not engage in the Bitcoin market via the dinky web interfaces the exchanges offer us, the "retail market" (small fish).

Bitcoin Whales

The large players being referred to are institutions such as Hedge Funds and Bitcoin Investment Funds. Some of these funds have announced their presence in the water:

- ❖ Pantera Capital
- ❖ Bitcoins Reserve
- ❖ Binary Financial
- ❖ Coin Capital Partners
- ❖ Falcon Global Capital
- ❖ Fortress
- ❖ Bitcoin Investment Trust
- ❖ Global Advisors Bitcoin Investment Fund

Others have yet to put oar to water...

- ❖ Bitcoin Index Fund

... and others may or may not exist, depending on your sources and the reach of your sonar.

These funds typically manage hundreds of thousands of bitcoins, which they strategically and covertly put through the exchanges via special arrangement – out of sight and obscured from regular retail traders.

With their large capital mass, institutions can move the market at will. It is here where the metaphor of a Bitcoin Whale comes into its own because any other inhabitant of the ocean must simply get out of the way, or be moved forcefully. Additionally, no current is strong enough to deflect the whale from its course, so its intention becomes the way.

Crypto Whales And How They Manipulate The Price

When you see a huge drop in a coins price, people will sometimes blame it on whales that are dumping on the market. Whales are people or possibly a group of people working together to hold a large percentage of that coin and can use this to their advantage to manipulate the price of a coin to the desired price. Typically when this occurs "weak hands" will start panic selling so they can buy back into the coin at a cheaper price. Not always does his tacit work in the whales favor.

If you been in the crypto world for awhile now i am sure you have heard of the term "Whale". The whale is the biggest creature in the ocean and for the most part can over power just about any other fish, so in crypto we refer to people or groups that have a large percent of a coins volume a whale. Coins that have a smaller total volume are a lot easier for a potential whale to manipulate.

Whales will use a tactic called rinse and repeat, this method can be extremely profitable to a whale if timed right. The holder with a large percentage of that coins volume starts selling off lower then the market rate, which in turn causes people to start panic selling. Then the whale will watch and re-buy back in when the price of the coin reaches a new low. Then just repeats this process accumulating more wealth, more coins, and more control over that coin.

Another way a whale can manipulate the price is by using buy and sell walls. If the coin drops people will generally start to buy in at a lower price and sell when it reaches a higher price. Makes sense. A whale has to have the actual funds to create the walls on the exchange. They can stack up either buy or sell walls and watch the price when it hits exactly where they want it then BOOM the wall disappears because they have canceled that large buy or sell order. There are actual real huge buy and sell walls that are not manipulated by whales. So you have to be careful, Don't get dumped on.

Whales don't always buy coins the traditional way through exchanges they can use Over the Counter Trading or Dark pools. This way they can buy vast amounts of a coin (if available) without it being noticed by the public eye. If you are a potential Whale you don't want the general public to notice your very large buy order all at one time. This would send signals to others that its getting ready to be manipulated. The great whale of 2014 caused an event where a massive liquidation of bitcoin where sold at 300 dollars a piece. Which was a supply of 30,000 bitcoins totaling 9 million dollars. People assumed this was going to crash the entire crypto market at the time, but to many people's surprise the buyers ripped right through the sell orders and the coin rose to $375 dollars.

So remember if you bought into a quality coin and believe in its community and tech, don't let weak hands deter you from staying in the game. Thousands of people have lost millions of dollars because of panic selling.

If you get involved playing with a whale and your trying to make huge gains HODL for Life!

Rinse and Repeat

There are many trading maneuvers whales use to profit, like using a trading tactlc commonly called the 'rinse and repeat cycle.' The rinse trade is used in many types of markets and can be effective if timed correctly and very profitable if you are a bitcoin whale. The trader with a lot of holdings starts selling bitcoins lower than the market rate which at times can cause a panic sell off by small-time traders. The trick is the whale sold just below the current market value and just enough to watch panic ensue. Then the whale waits and watches the panic selling take place until the bitcoin price reaches a new low. At this point, the whales quickly scoop up way more bitcoins than they first started with and after the 'rinse' they usually 'repeat' this type of trade often. People speculate that there are many ways whales can throw their 'BTC weight' around to either push the price up or down to accumulate more bitcoins. Further, whales are not just individuals and can be an organization like a bitcoin investment fund as well.

Bitcoin Liquidity

By injecting, say, 50,000 BTC, over the course of a week, a massive price change can be effected. Yet, doing so, for its own sake is pointless because the institution's objective, just like smaller players, is to buy low and sell high – in other words, to turn a profit after each investment.

Buying 1 BTC now and selling a split-second later results in a trading loss due to the spread between the buy and sell prices. Let's increase the amount of BTC in this example: buying, say, 10,000 BTC all in one go, and assuming the exchange could absorb that amount, would not only move the market price, it would also trigger ask orders on the way up, as well as see many participants take profit at higher levels.

Hence, large market transactions are appropriate for exiting trades, but not for initiating them, since the effect of spread and of triggering "obstacle" limit orders reduces the net effect of large orders in the market. Instead, the largest players have to stagger and obscure their market entries by splitting large trades into hundreds or thousands of small orders and then drip these into the market over hours, days or weeks.

This Way, Please

Given the institution's desire to maximize the profitability of a large trade it initiates, it would increase the distance that this trade travels if the institution can have retailers (the small fish) join them in the move.

Hence, the largest players have no choice, but to "prime" the market: to read wider market conditions, assess the retail sector's "mood" and the willingness of market participants to go in a particular direction.

Once an opportunity is identified, the task is then to "massage" the market and steer participants in the desired direction. The institutional player, therefore, achieves a greater return on investment – the investment having been the expenditure of setting up and "massaging" a particular move – and the outcome of the move being that small retailers and new public participants had taken the bait and herded into the rally, thereby increasing its market impact and slingshot effect.

Market-wide phenomenon

If any reader thinks that this sounds incredible, be assured that this is not my proposal of how I think it works, it's standard hedge fund practice. Large banks, the market makers for most of the Forex market, have teams of traders dedicated to doing just this via trade plans that last anywhere from a day to a few weeks.

The Bitcoin market has several characteristics that make it ideal for high risk institutional investors like hedge funds:

- ❖ Small market capitalization
- ❖ Relatively naive participants
- ❖ No bank competitors
- ❖ No regulation

The institutions listed have apparently become active in the Bitcoin market during the course of the past two years. While there is no sense in speaking of collusion, it seems only rational that large players should (at least, sometimes) coordinate their actions. Given that there are community members who are known to hold sizable amounts of Bitcoin, one could imagine that they would reasonably discuss and align their interests with other potential market movers.

So, it's not about that 1000 BTC order you see in the exchange orderbook, or the 50 BTC that went through Dell's online retail store today. The BTC market, although high-risk and based on an innovation that's difficult to fathom, is a speculator's wildest dream come true. All the time while it is adjusting downwards, it's because the largest players are herding the bait-ball.

As for the small Bitcoin fish it's most beneficial to just swim with the Bitcoin whale and swim away when the mood starts getting frenzied near the surface. Knowing what time it is, is the challenge.

Whales Are Often Blamed for Big Market Shake Outs

Whales have been discussed in the bitcoin space for quite some time, and they are usually blamed for unexplainable market phenomenon. Further, there are a lot of conversations across bitcoin forums asking the question — How many bitcoins does it take to be a whale? It seems the answer varies from 1,000 bitcoins to 10,000 bitcoins according to multiple threads on Bitcointalk.org and Reddit. Many people believe that whales can still affect the market due to bitcoin's relatively small market capitalization where multi-million dollar orders can still shake things up. As bitcoin markets become stronger and gain more liquidity, speculators believe it now takes bigger bitcoin whales to shift the trading waters.

HOW TO BUY ETHEREUM

Purchasing Ethereum can be done easily at any Ethereum exchanges. Once Ether has been purchased for fiat currency (USD, EUR, GBP etc), the funds can be stored on the exchange itself or in your own secure wallet. For small purchases of Ethereum, users may wish to store their crypto on the exchange for ease-of-use. For larger purchases it is recommended that the funds are moved into a secure wallet. Alternatively, investors can trade Ethereum without having to buy and secure the currency through a CFD trading platform such as eToro.

Purchasing Ethereum from an exchange

The process of purchasing Ethereum through an exchange is simple. Register an account with an exchange, deposit US dollars, Euros etc and purchase Ether through the platform.

If you would prefer to just speculate on the price of Ether without purchasing the cryptoasset (and thus not requiring any of the associated security precautions).

Buy Ether in a few simple steps

The process of buying Ether will vary from exchange to exchange, however the principles are very much the same. Those new to currency purchases need not be alarmed, many exchange platforms make it as easy as sending a single online payment.

1. Register at an exchange

Register at your chosen exchange by submitting a few personal details. Full identity checks are often included later in the process when a deposit or withdrawal is made.

2. Complete KYC/identity checks

Before/after depositing, or prior to withdrawal, exchanges must carry out "Know Your Customer" (KYC) and Anti-

Money Laundering (AML) checks. Exchanges will require proof of address and photo identification to proceed.

3. Choose a deposit method

Each Ethereum exchange will offer their own banking methods. These are often a mix of bank wire transfers, SEPA, credit/debit card or PayPal payments. Each exchange will typically charge a fee for each deposit method; fee details are usually found in the footer of the exchange's website.

4. Make a deposit in US dollars, Euros etc

Deposits will take from as little as 24 hours to several days to arrive in your exchange account. Deposit times will vary from exchange to exchange and the deposit method chosen.

5. Buy Ether with your deposited funds

Once your fiat currency has arrived in your exchange account, you can use this currency to purchase Ether. Beginner friendly platforms such as Coinbase have made this process very simple.

How to Buy Ethereum: An Intro to Ethereum Investment

Ethereum is a blockchain – a ledger containing a history of all transactions – that is secured by a distributed network of machines, each working to process and validate transactions. Ether, the currency of the Ethereum blockchain, is issued to those machines that carry out this work, and Ether can then be traded easily for fiat currencies like US dollars or Euros. This network now has many thousands of participants who are able to transact with anyone in the world without middlemen.

Transactions on Ethereum are final and immutable. If a transaction is invalid (for example, the user does not have enough funds), then the transaction is not included in the blockchain. The entire history of all valid transactions is stored by many different machines in thousands of physical locations, each copy being identical to the other. The blockchain is a global agreement of the history of every transaction ever made. Due to this distributed nature of the Ethereum blockchain, there is no central point of failure and no possibility of being shut down.

The Ethereum blockchain was launched in July 2015 with a price of less than a dollar and climbed slowly until March 2017 when the cryptoasset experienced an enormous surge in price. This guide to buying Ethereum will explain why Ether has value, whether the currency is a good investment, and what risks and considerations should be taken into account when looking to buy Ether.

To first understand Ethereum's value proposition, and whether you as an investor should consider purchasing Ether, it is best to consider the unique benefits that cryptoassets offer and why they attract the attention of such a broad range of investors, from VCs through to retail.

Purchasing Ether Anonymously

Some may prefer a "peer to peer" route to purchasing Ethereum, avoiding KYC and AML and in many cases, purchasing larger quantities. Whilst this activity may be frowned upon by your country's regulators, it is possible to do so – at your own risk – through an online peer to peer exchange like LocalBitcoins.com

This route first requires the purchase of Bitcoin, which is then exchanged for Ether. Setting up a Bitcoin wallet is much the same as the process above, and a list of trusted wallets can be found on Bitcoin.org.

Bitcoin can then be exchanged for Ether anonymously through ShapeShift.io. However each transaction is limited to a maximum amount (typically a few thousand dollars in value).

Definitions

Before discussing Ethereum as an alternative investment vehicle and its many benefits, risks and rewards, it is best to list a handful of definitions which should help make this steps easier to follow.

➢ **Cryptoasset**

General term for any asset secured by cryptography, predominantly blockchain-based assets like Ethereum and Bitcoin.

➢ **Fiat currency**

Legal tender such as US dollars, Euros or British Pounds.

➢ **Market cap**

Is the total value of coin supply multiplied by the price per coin. A general term used to roughly quantify the value of an entire network.

➢ **Exchange**

A platform used to buy and sell cryptoassets.

➤ Smart contracts

An immutable set of instructions (written in code) that execute autonomously. An example would be a flight insurance smart contract; this would automatically release funds to relevant parties based on whether a flight was delayed using trusted 3rd party flight data as the "truthsayer" or "oracle".

➤ Ethereum Virtual Machine (EVM)

A term for the Ethereum blockchain, specifically referencing its computational ability and use of smart contracts.

➤ Ethereum node

A machine with a complete copy of the Ethereum blockchain. The Ethereum network consists of many thousands of nodes, each verifying every transactions in the blockchain.

➤ Ethereum miner

A machine that bundles transactions into "blocks" and adds them to the blockchain. Blocks are added to the chain when the miner is able to successfully complete a difficult computational problem.

Why is Ethereum valuable?

Unlike other assets, Ethereum is not backed by gold or promised by government. To understand whether Ethereum is worth buying, it is first best to examine the fundamental value of the Ethereum blockchain itself. For the sake of simplicity, this section will look at the Ethereum blockchain only.

Mathematics and scarcity

The Ethereum blockchain is a protocol that operates on the laws of mathematics. Unlike a central bank or government, who can quickly and unexpectedly adjust money supply, Ethereum's coin distribution is written into immutable code that is publicly available and agreed by consensus. It is the blockchain's unbreakable encryption and mathematical truths which back this digital asset, as opposed to gold or government promise.

Ethereum is an inflationary currency; 5 new Ether coins enter the system whenever the next valid block in the blockchain is found (a block is found roughly every 15 seconds). The process of finding blocks is a separate topic, but the key point is that – unlike Bitcoin, whose supply is capped at 21 million coins – there is no limit on the amount of Ether that will be issued over time. However, this rate of inflation will decrease over time as the aforementioned issuance of 5 Ether becomes a smaller percentage of the overall coin supply. Furthermore, planned network changes (which must be agreed by consensus), due to be launched in the coming months, will place downward pressure on the inflation rate.

Sovereignty

Transactions on the Ethereum blockchain are valid based on a few factors, but the most obvious is that the user must have a balance greater than the amount they are sending. The purpose for which they are sending or receiving coins is irrelevant. Any user of the Ethereum blockchain – regardless of location – is able to decide how to spend their value without authorization. Having sovereignty over one's wealth may seem unnecessary for many in the West, however those from developing nations, or countries experiencing hyper inflation and money controls, stand to benefit enormously by untethering from their fiat currency system. Unlike the traditional fiat system, Ethereum offers users full sovereignty if they wish. Of course users can choose to trust 3rd parties if they would like to, but that is not a requirement as it is in the traditional banking space today.

Efficiency

Ethereum transactions are low cost and fast, capable of handling 15 transactions per second with protocol upgrades in the next 12 months that are anticipated to increase this figure to 1000+. To put that into perspective, VISA handles an estimated average of 2,000 transactions per second. Furthermore, 3rd party payment channels are being developed which will take transactions off of the Ethereum blockchain without compromising security and reducing fees further – increasing the capacity of the network by several orders of magnitude.

Liquidity

Ether has real-world value that is in demand. Major Ethereum exchanges will complete large million dollar sell orders within seconds without moving the price. Liquidity could certainly be higher, and brief "flash crashes" have been noted in the past, however for the vast majority of users and investors,

Ethereum's liquidity allows for fast exchange to and from fiat currency.

Ethereum Virtual Machine (EVM)

Up until now we have focused on the fundamentals of the Ethereum blockchain and its use case as a currency for transacting value. Ether serves well as a currency, however it is the ability to deploy "smart contracts" on the EVM which furthers its case as an alternative investment. Smart contracts are still in their infancy, however a number of industries are on the cusp of major disruption thanks to this technology:

- ❖ Prediction markets
- ❖ Gambling
- ❖ Insurance
- ❖ Trading

Much like gold, Ethereum and others are being used as a hedge against economic uncertainty. However unlike gold, Ether can also be transacted globally and near-instantaneously through the internet with minimal fees and unlimited amounts. The supply of Ethereum is also transparent and predictable through its open source code which is publicly auditable. In the case of gold, supply shocks are not uncommon.

Why invest in Ethereum?

There are several reasons why a user might choose to buy or invest In Ethereum, here a handful of examples.

Buying Ethereum as an investment

- ❖ Accessing token sales and other blockchain investments
- ❖ Hedging against the incumbent fiat system
- ❖ Diversifying a traditional portfolio

Buying Ethereum for use

- ❖ Interacting with blockchain-based IoT devices
- ❖ Using smart contracts and the EVM
- ❖ Paying wages internationally

What investment strategy?

Investment strategies vary, and suitability is subject to your own personal risk tolerance. This guide is for information purposes only, and if in any doubt consult a financial adviser.

Buy and hold

One of the most common investment strategies for Ethereum is "buy and hold". If Ethereum is to replace even a fraction of fiat currency, its value will be far greater than it is today. The same can be said if Ethereum becomes the currency of choice for the "machine payable web" which will enable billions of devices to transact value efficiently with each other.

Given the volatility of Ethereum, those looking to buy may want to consider "dollar cost averaging"; spending the total investment amount in chunks over X period of time to acquire Ether at an averaged price.

Buy and diversify

It is safe to say that predicting the future of Ethereum is much like predicting the weather in 5 years time. It is unlikely that Ethereum will disappear anytime soon, but as Ethereum has shown Bitcoin, it is possible for a little-known cryptoasset to become a dominant force in a short period of time. Purchasing Ethereum to exchange for other cryptoassets like Ripple (XRP) and Ethereum Classic (ETC) is a good way to hedge against the unexpected failure of any given coin. Whilst one coin may fail, many VCs and technologists are in agreement that cryptoassets of some nature will become ubiquitous in the future.

Ethereum trading

Some investors choose to day trade cryptoassets on exchanges like Poloniex and GDAX. This type of trading compounds risk on an already volatile asset and should be treated with caution. Let's not go there.

Is it too late to buy Ethereum?

If Ethereum was to become ubiquitous as a digital currency – enabling micropayments among machines and borderless/trustless transactions between people – then it is quite obviously not too late to buy Ethereum. The price of Ethereum in 10 years time is likely to either be $0.00 or an uncapped amount that can only be imagined. It is my personal expectation that Ethereum's value will only stabalize (i.e. stop increasing) once the currency has achieved its goal of being a globally decentralized platform with billions of devices and humans interacting with it. Of course, the value of the currency will experience enormous highs and lows as investors join and whales leave, but if the technology is to succeed, then the long run price will be much greater than today.

From the content on this book, it should also become apparent just how challenging it can be to purchase Ether, and that in and of itself is one reason why it is unlikely to be too late.

Ethereum wallets

Before purchasing Ether, it's essential to become familiar with wallet software and transactions in general. Ethereum – as with any cryptoasset – is extremely unforgiving. One false move when sending or receiving a transaction can result in the loss of an entire bankroll. However, this risk can be somewhat mitigated. The risk can be further mitigated by learning a basic understanding of the technology in this section (it's not complex) and using caution.

An Ethereum wallet is a piece of software that "stores" your Ether funds. Ethereum wallets could be a desktop application, a mobile/web app, a hardware/paper wallet or an online exchange. The official Ethereum wallet can be downloaded at Ethereum.org.

Light client or "full node"?

New users may find themselves downloading a "full node". Full nodes can be used as a wallet, however they require the user to download the full Ethereum blockchain (many gigabytes in size). If you are new to Ethereum, then it is recommended that you use a "light client". Light clients do not require the full blockchain to operate.

Light client Ethereum wallets:

- ❖ MyEtherWallet
- ❖ Jaxx.io (also supports other cryptoassets)

Private key

Now that you have chosen a particular Ethereum wallet, it is important to understand the private key that will be generated with it before depositing any funds. The private key is the key to your wallet; if anyone else has your private key then they also have full access to your wallet and its associated funds. When creating a wallet, you will be asked to take a copy of your private key. The above wallets generate your private key offline, it is never sent to a server and therefore cannot be intercepted. It is now up to you how to store and backup your private key. Many users choose secure cloud storage with 2-factor authentication or offline prints of their private key. For larger sums of Ethereum, extra security measures can be taken with "hardware wallets" described further in the book.

Transactions and addresses

You have now downloaded an Ethereum wallet and secured your private key. Before funding your wallet with Ether, it's important to become familiar with the make-up of a simple Ethereum transaction.

Your Ethereum wallet will automatically generate a handful of receiving addresses (also known as "public keys") which are a function of your private key. Unlike the private key, receiving addresses can be distributed freely without risk of theft, and payments to these receiving addresses will add funds to your private key (wallet).

All transactions on the Ethereum blockchain are publicly visible through a "block explorer" such as Etherscan.io. As an example, we are going to look at this arbitrary transaction of 0.2 ETH. In this transaction you can see 2 public keys:

From:
0xea674fdde714fd979de3edf0f56aa9716b898ec8

To:
0x3d167984ae0868194ffd97759ff74e342ff3140d

Using MyEtherWallet for example, a transaction is simply the input of the address we wish to send funds to, the amount, and the gas limit (fee). The latter is set automatically by the software – but it's prudent to double check the cost as miscalculations have been known to occur.

The from address does not need to be specified. This address is chosen automatically based on the balance of each address.

Once a transaction has been sent, a transaction hash is created and shown to you in the software. This transaction hash can then be put into a block explorer and the same details we have just looked at can be found for your new transaction.

Block height and confirmations

This is the mined block which your transaction was included in. It takes roughly 15 seconds to mine a block. The period between your transaction being broadcast (i.e. sent to a receiving address) to when it is first included in a block is a period in which your transaction will be "pending". Inclusion in a block is called a confirmation, and every subsequently mined block adds another confirmation. The more confirmations a transaction has, the more "bedded-into" the blockchain it is. Transactions with 30+ confirmations are generally considered extremely secure – they will persist in the blockchain for all eternity.

Block height can also be thought of as the block number since the creation of the blockchain.

Receiving transactions

Now that you are familiar with sending Ether, the same idea can be applied to receiving it. In the case of purchasing Ethereum, once it has been bought from an exchange, the exchange's withdrawal function will ask for your wallet address. Input your address along with the amount of Ether you wish to withdraw to your wallet, and then once confirmed, a transaction hash will be shown. The Ether will immediately show as being "pending" in your wallet, and you can follow the number of confirmations it has using the transaction hash on Etherscan.io.

Transacting Ethereum safely

Whilst rare, there have been several horror stories of users losing thousands of dollars in Ether from poor due diligence. Here are a few of the key items to check off when making a transaction of a significant sum.

Copy and paste the address

Never type in a wallet address by hand. Addresses are long and case-sensitive, a single mistake will result in the funds being lost forever. There is no charge back or customer support number in Ethereum.

Check the transaction fee

A good Ethereum wallet will show you the calculated transaction fee in dollars and cents. Always double check that the transaction fee is reasonable.

Check, double and triple check the address

Once you've copied and pasted the address which you wish to send or receive Ether to, check it over and over until you're certain it's correct. Looking at the first and last several letters/numbers will ensure it's been pasted correctly.

Good wallet software will also confirm the address that you are sending or receiving to. This mitigates the risk of malware intercepting and replacing the address you input.

Test your transaction

One of the driving forces behind Ethereum adoption is the low transaction fees. There is no harm in sending a negligible amount of Ether in order to test your understanding of the process and that all of the details are correct. This will ensure that everything goes smoothly when sending larger amounts.

Securing Ethereum – the easy way

This method of security hands over management to the exchange with which you purchased Ether.

In this instance, users can secure their newly purchased Ethereum by leaving it in their wallet on the exchange itself. This introduces some risks, Including platform risk (the platform may fail as has been seen before with the MtGox Bitcoin exchange) as well as the risk of digital theft, as was seen with Bitfinex. Ultimately, some users choose to secure large sums of Ether by leaving it on an exchange, but in doing so they give up their ability to audit and ensure its security. The decision to do this is a personal one – how much do you trust the exchange, and how much are you willing to leave in the hands of that exchange? Whilst it is unlikely that your coins will be stolen, or that platform will become insolvent, it is a real possibility that should be accounted for.

A note on exchanges

Securing Ether on an exchange is a legitimate approach to security, particularly if the funds stored are relatively small in size compared to an investor's overall portfolio. However, when storing coins on an exchange, you do not own the private key. Essentially, you have handed over responsibility of your Ether to the exchange. Exchanges are not the same as a bank, and the same financial regulations do not apply. Insolvency or theft may result in lost funds.

Securing Ethereum – the hard way

Securing Ether is a critical step in ensuring that your investment is safe. Unlike many developed countries, the banks will not protect your cryptoassets like they protect your cash. As mentioned, investing in cryptocurrencies in unforgiving, securing Ether properly is critical. Those looking for a simpler security option by handing over this management to a 3rd party can see the above section.

Securing Ethereum through a hardware wallet

Hardware wallets are one of the safest ways to secure your Ether. Hardware wallets generate and store your private key offline, and at no point is the private key exposed to your connected device (PC). Storing your coins offline in this way mitigates the risk of digital theft – one of the most common attack vectors for cryptoasset holders. As with other Ethereum wallets, a recovery seed is provided on creation, and a PIN is chosen to secure access to the device itself. It is the PIN and the recovery seed that must then be secured extremely well, as access to either by a malicious individual may result in loss of funds. Further protection can also be taken in the form of 2-factor authentication and multi-signature wallets.

The two most respected hardware wallets for Ethereum (and other cryptoassets) are Trezor and the Ledger Nano S. Those storing Ethereum on a Trezor device will need to use it in combination with MyEtherWallet (see the full guide here). For that reason, many users opt for the ease of use that comes with the Ledger Nano

Additional security measures you can take

2 Factor Authentication

Whether you choose to store your coins on an exchange, desktop/mobile wallet or hardware wallet, 2 Factor Authentication (2FA) is a highly recommended additional security layer. The 2FA process requires that the user inputs a one time password (OTP) before being able to login to a wallet or send Ether. Google Authenticator is one of the most popular interfaces for 2FA and is used by a range of Ethereum wallets.

Different wallets and exchanges will implement 2FA in different ways, however the additional security that it provides remains the same. A potential thief would not only require your password to steal your Ether, but access to the physical device from which the OTP is generated as well.

A word of caution

2FA through an app like Google Authenticator has so far proven extremely secure. However, some platforms choose to bypass the use of an app and instead send an OTP over SMS. SMS 2FA should be avoided entirely, as the OTP can – in many cases – be observed without needing to unlock a phone. More catastrophically, social engineering has been used to convince telecoms staff to port a phone number to a new SIM; if an attacker is able to do this, then the phone number alone can be used to gain access to any platform "protected" by SMS 2FA.

Multi Signature Wallets

These wallets allow the user to secure their Ethereum by requiring multiple participants to sign each transaction. Typically a multi signature wallet is "2 of 3", meaning that 2 of a total of 3 private keys must sign the transaction for it to be successfully broadcast to the network. In these instances, the 3 private keys can be split across different physical locations along with their own physical security to ensure that there is no single point of attack.

Different wallets will have their own implementations of multi signature security.

Extra Security Layers

Ultimately, the security options that you choose should be based around your risk tolerance. Cryptoasset security practices are being developed on an ongoing basis, consult your wallet of choice for their own recommendations.